BLACK LIKE WATER

*A Collection of Poems, Spells, Recipes
and Writing Prompts*

Sincerely Shyy

AOS Publishing, 2024

Shiann Croft

ISBN: 978-1-998662-22-7

Cover Design: Meredith Lindsay

Visit AOS Publishing's website:
www.aospublishing.com

Dedication

This book is dedicated to Guyana, my momma,
Allyson Adley, my uncle Keith and my aunties—
Aunty Michelle, Aunty Donna, and Aunty Jennifer—
whose strength flows through me like a river.
It is their voice I hear when I call on my ancestors,
their love that has shaped me,
and their resilience that pushes me forward.

To them, this journey is as much ours as it is mine.
Their wisdom, their sacrifices,
their unwavering belief,
is the foundation on which I stand.

May this river we've built together never run dry.

Table of Contents

Black Like Water 1

Prelude: The River Begins 4

Section One: Guyana, The Waters of Our Beginning 8

We Rise, We Roar 9

Praise for the Work 10

I Am That Which I Am 11

The River of Reclamation 12

The River of My People: A Letter to Sousedyke 13

The Ocean Remembers 14

Revolution Is a River: Dear Land of Guyana.................. 15

Water of Rebellion: A Letter to the Demerara.............. 17

Recipe: The Waters of Healing 19

Recipe: Ancient Waters for the Soul 20

Writing Prompt: The Revolution Runs Through Your Veins........ 21

Meditation: Flow Like the River............................... 22

Section Two: The Return to Ourselves 23

Introduction: The Return to Ourselves 24

The Sacredness of My Skin... 25

Resilience in My Bones... 26

The Mirror Speaks 27

Nyah Ndidi 28

Africa 29

Reclaiming the Power of Our Bodies 30

Recipe: Nourish the Temple... 31

**Section Three: Feminine Power, Sexuality,
and the Sacred Body** 32

Breathless: Love in the Time of Revolution 33

Dancing in Our Skin 35

Unforgiven 36

Soft Revolutions 38

Sacred Touch, Sacred Fury... 39

Still I Rise: A Black Girl's Love Song................................. 40

Writing Prompts:... 41

Sister, Your Body is Not for Their Consumption 42

The Power of Unapologetic Desire: Black Feminist Thoughts 43

Breathe, Girl 45

Writing Prompt: Sister, Reclaim Your Sacredness 47

The Sacred Rage 48

Touch Me... 49

**Section Four: The Reclamation of Covens and the
Rise of Black Spirituality** 51

The Return of the Healers: Our Magic is Not New........... 52

Coven in the Bones.. 53

Sis.. 54

Black Girl Magic is Not an Aesthetic 55

My Sister's Keeper... 56

Black Girl, Call Home: SOS... 58

Radical Herbal Recipes 60

The Recipe For Resistance 61

Bloodroot Balm.. 62

The Daughters of the Healers 63

The Role of the Black Feminist Witch 64

Witchcraft is Not a Fantasy, It Is a Revolution.................... 65

The Power of Remembering.. 67

Black Like Water 68

Reflection: 69

Exercise: Claim Your Space 70

Closing Reflection: 71

Black Like Water

I am Black like water—
Not the trickle of fear,
Not the soft murmur of a song unsung.
I am the flood,
I am the wave,
I am the river that carved history
into the bones of this earth.

I am the river that does not ask for permission
to rise,
to overflow,
to tear through your walls
and drown your silence.

I am Black like my mother —
I carry the weight of the days we've fought,
the blood that soaked the soil
of lands you tried to steal.
The sun shone too brightly for you to claim us,
but still you tried,
and I,
Black like water,
washed your lies away.

I am Black like water—
They thought they could chain me,
tie me down to their names and their borders,
but I flowed through their fingers like sand.
You see,
water don't know boundaries.
It don't know oppression.

It don't know borders
because water was made before words.

I am Black like water—
I flowed over the Middle Passage,
crashed against the shores of your ignorance.
I am the salt in your wound,
the tear in your eye,
the one you call 'other' but can't live without.
I carried your forefathers' sins
in my belly,
and still,
I rose.

I am Black like water—
I washed the dust from the feet of our elders,
stood tall when they tried to bury us in the shadows of your
history.
I was there when you built your cities on stolen land.
I was there when you burned the villages,
raped the earth.
I watched as you bent the trees to your will,
but Black like water,
I don't bend.

I am Black like water—
I am the fire that burns in the belly of the earth.
The song of the drum that echoes through your bones.
I am the sound of the rivers rising
when you thought you could drown us.
I am the breath you thought you stole,
now filling my lungs,
and I speak in tongues of my own making.

I am Black like water—
I am the breath of liberation,
the pulse in the heart of revolution.
I am the body you tried to erase
but found waiting in the reflections.
I am the one who rises again,
and again,
and again.

I am Black like water—
You thought you could name me,
contain me,
but I am the moon's call to the tides.
I am the deep,
the shallow,
the storm,
the calm.

I am Black like water—
You cannot cage me,
you cannot name me,
you cannot drown me,
for I am the very current that runs through your veins,
the storm in your chest
when you can't breathe because the weight of your own guilt
crushes your chest.

I am Black like water—
and I will wash you clean.

Prelude:
The River Begins

We were born from water.
The Earth itself, shaped by water, cradled in the womb of the oceans.
Water carved valleys, sculpted mountains, and held the world in its embrace.
Water is not gentle.
It is the origin of life and the force that demands we rise.

Before you were born, before your ancestors breathed air,
before time had a name, there was water.
The current that moved through the earth is the same one that runs through your veins.
You are the river that carried the stories.
You are the deep—unseen, untamed.

Water doesn't ask permission.
Water takes what it needs,
it shapes and it moves,
and it does this without apology.
It is fluid and it is fierce.
You are this.
You are water.

Black Like Water is not just a book.
It's a declaration.
A resurrection.
It's the invitation to step back into your power,
to step back into the fullness of your Blackness,
to reclaim your body as sacred,
your love as revolutionary,

your presence as unshakable.

In a world that tries to drown us,
tries to make us small,
tries to diminish us in every corner,
yet we are still here.
We are the flood that won't be held back.
We are the river that will never run dry.

This is the beginning of something deep.
You were never meant to shrink into the shadows.
You were meant to stand tall,
to stand unapologetically,
and to flow in the power that is your birthright.

Black Like Water isn't just a collection of words; it is an
invitation to *transform*.
The stories inside these pages are not just to be read.
They are meant to be felt in your body,
in the rhythm of your pulse,
in the breath that moves through you.
These words are the wind that moves the waters of your soul.

But this isn't a passive process.
This is a revolution that requires your participation.
You are called to step into the current,
to wade through your own history,
to wash away the remnants of shame,
the remnants of silence,
the remnants of a world that tried to define you.

Black Like Water is about healing, but it's also about
reclaiming.
Reclaiming the sacredness of your body,
your lineage,

your love.
Reclaiming the stories that were stolen from us,
the rhythms of our ancestors that still pulse beneath our skin.

This is an invitation to move, to act,
to break free from the chains of conformity,
to live unapologetically,
to step into your power,
to hold your space in a world that constantly seeks to take it from you.

This book is for every Black Caribbean woman who has ever been told her body was too much, too loud, too dark. For every Black woman who has been told she doesn't belong, that her love is dangerous, that her power is a threat. For every woman who has been forced to shrink in order to survive in a world that was never built for her.

This book is for you.
It is for those who are ready to rise, ready to reclaim what was always theirs,
to find their joy and their freedom,
to love their bodies and their truths.

Healing is not an individual act.
It is a collective uprising.
When we heal, we heal together.
When we rise, we rise as a people.
This book is about the community that surrounds you,
the ancestors that walk with you,
the sisters and mothers who will carry you through.

You are the river.
The river is you.

Black Like Water is a call to step into the water,
to flow with it,
to allow it to reshape you.
It is a call to recognize your own divinity,
to honor your body as sacred,
to feel the full force of your power,
and to rise.

In the beginning, there was water.
In the beginning, there was *you*.
And everything that came before you,
and everything that will come after you,
is carried by the current that flows through you.

You are the river.
You are the storm.
You are the flood that will change the world.

So step in.
The revolution has already begun.

Section One

Guyana, The Waters of Our Beginning

A Deep Dive into Ancestral Memory, History, and Reclamation

We Rise, We Roar

Let the world remember the sound
of a Black woman's voice—
not whispering, not pleading,
but **roaring**.
Let the heavens tremble at the fire
we have carried in our wombs,
in our skin,
in our bones,
for centuries.
No more quiet prayers
to gods who do not know us.
We will paint the sky with our cries,
wrap our rage in wings
and make **the revolution**
the song we sing.
We rise from the ashes
of forgotten histories.
We rise from the weight
of all that was meant to break us.
We rise
and we rise
and we rise
until the sun bows to our light.

Praise for the Work

Praise for the story and the purpose,
Praise, for heavy is the crown, praise, for heavy is the burden.
Praise Jah for all of the becoming,
the lessons learned, the journey between getting lost and finding
the way,
only to do it all over again.
Praise for the all-over-again.
Praise Jah, for this is the work, this is the sanctuary.
This right here is healing, these words are my offerings,
this right here is holy.
This is a secret gathering in the dead of midnight—now snap if
you feel me.
Snap for the ones that did not get a chance to.
Snap for the elders that whispered, prayed, conjured up ancestors
from the mud.
Praise for the blood, black blood in these veins,
I am hand-clapped roti,
I am magical concoctions of oils and hymns and praise.
I am red lavender and black obsidian,
I am Huey P Newton born again in divine feminine.
I am deletions of sacred texts from the Book of Enoch,
I am the amen before and after the utterance of a prayer—this
right here is holy.
Don't approach this goddess without offerings;
I said this right here is holy.
The sucking of teeth and patios that we speak when we talk that
talk is holy.
The joy of black boys walking down the block with a strut and a
sway—
it is hip hop, it is rhythm, and the rhythm is ours and it is holy.
The way that we wine our waist and go down in the rain,
it is an ancient dance and it is holy.

I Am That Which I Am

Who are you? they ask, and I respond with,
I AM THAT WHICH I AM.
I don't believe in labels or man-made religions;
The universe is my teacher, my heart the temple.
I was created in the image of the creator.
I AM melanin.
I AM substance.
I AM negative pressure rising.
I AM carbon, I am hydrogen
I AM the divine elements of this Earth.
I AM Shiann.
I AM THAT WHICH I AM.
What do you believe in? they ask.
I reject all images of a white Christ.
I believe in the unification of my people.
I am neither Pan-African nor pro-black;
Even though I am these things, I am so much more.
I AM THAT WHICH I AM.
I AM a reflection of God herself.
I AM black consciousness.
I AM divine feminine.
As I put this pen to paper,
It's hard to find the right words, adjectives, or verbs to describe me.
How can you define a Goddess when a Goddess cannot be
contained?
Just know that
I AM THAT WHICH I SAY I AM.
My soul is connected to the abundance of the universe,
Which makes me immortal.
I know it's hard for your simple mind to understand,
So next time you ask me who I am,
Just know that
I AM THAT WHICH I AM.

The River of Reclamation

The river has always been our guide,
a path carved by those who came before us—
who lived in its flow,
who resisted its damming.
From the shores of Africa to the rivers of the Americas,
we carry the water of our ancestors in our bones.
It is the river of rebellion,
of survival,
of memory.

This is a journey through the waters of our beginning.
Through the stories we've carried,
the history we've inherited,
and the revolution we are still rising to.
The river does not forget.
And neither do we.

The River of My People:
A Letter to Sousedyke

I come from the river,
where the waters do not ask permission
to carve it's path.
They tried to name it—
but it was never theirs to own.
The river carries the names
of those who were stolen,
those who fought,
those who drowned but never disappeared.
I carry them.
I am not just blood and bone,
I am water.
I am the river that flows through you,
through your mother,
through your mother's mother,
and beyond.
I am the answer to the question:
Where do you come from?
I come from the river that cannot be tamed.

The Ocean Remembers

The ocean remembers,
its waves whispering secrets to the shore—
of those who crossed it,
the ones who didn't make it,
and the ones who did.
It is in the salt of the sea
and the deep pull of the tides
that I know my history—
my bloodline is ancient,
older than the cities they built on stolen land.

We are not new.
We are not born from nothing.
We are from the ocean,
from the flood that comes when the earth remembers its rage.
And I, too, remember that I am the daughter of the ocean.

Revolution Is a River:
Dear Land of Guyana

I was born in a river of fire
and water.
Do you hear it?
The river hums songs of freedom,
struggles etched in the bones of my grandmothers
who fought with fire in their hands and earth in their feet.
They passed that flame to me.
I carry it in my blood,
in the marrow of my bones,
in the rise of my breath.

Revolution is a river,
a current so deep
you can't drown it.
You can only flow with it.
Let me tell you,
the river don't stop
because they dammed it with fear.
The river don't stop
because they named it sin.
The river don't stop
because they tried to erase the water's tongue—
we speak in the language of struggle,
we speak in the language of survival.

So I rise, like my grandmothers before me.
The river in me is a march,
not just a flow.
My feet know the rhythm of resistance,
the pulse of power under this skin.

I am the river,
and the river cannot be contained.
So hear me—
The flood is coming.
The storm is gathering.
And you can try to silence the water,
but I promise you,
we'll rise.

Water of Rebellion:
A Letter to the Demerara

Water was the first rebellion.
Before chains were forged,
before names were stolen,
before we were taught to hate our own reflection,
there was water.
It flowed in the bodies of our ancestors—
carrying stories of revolt, of resilience,
of life and death.
It carved paths through history
that no human could erase,
no matter how hard they tried.
This is the truth we carry in our bones.

Water is our inheritance.
The river that carries us from Africa to the Americas,
from the Caribbean to the shores of freedom,
is the same river that runs through our blood.
We are descendants of the flood,
of the wave,
of the storm that cannot be contained.

But let us not forget—
water is not just a body of liquid.
Water is a memory.
Water is the spirit of survival.
Water does not ask permission to rise.
It does not care for borders, for chains, for laws.
It simply flows.
It knows no fear.
It knows no limits.

I am Black like water.
Endless, deep, untamable.
I rise in the same way the river rises—
unapologetic, unbroken, a constant force of nature.

Recipe:
The Waters of Healing

Ingredients:

- 2 cups of spring water
- 1 tablespoon of sea salt
- 1 teaspoon of honey
- A handful of fresh mint leaves
- A few slices of ginger root

Instructions:

In a large glass bowl, pour in the spring water,
allowing it to breathe, to remember its origin.
Add the sea salt, remembering that salt is both a preservative and a
purifier. Let it dissolve.
Drop in the honey, the sweetness of resistance, the sweetness of
survival.
Add the fresh mint leaves, grounding yourself in the knowledge
that we are rooted in the earth,
even when the winds try to blow us off course.
Slice the ginger root, letting its sharpness remind you of the
power in every step.
Stir the mixture with your hands, honoring the water and all that
it carries.
As you stir, close your eyes and remember your ancestors.
Drink deeply, feeling the water heal you,
feeling the current of your history running through you, forever
alive.

Recipe:
Ancient Waters for the Soul

Ingredients:

- 1 cup of coconut water
- 2 tablespoons of turmeric
- 1/2 teaspoon of black pepper
- 1 tablespoon of raw cacao
- A pinch of cinnamon

Instructions:

In a small pot, heat the coconut water until it is warm but not boiling—this is a time for stillness.

Stir in the turmeric, a golden root that speaks of the sun, the strength, and the ancient power of the earth.

Add the black pepper, grounding the power of the turmeric in the body.

Add the raw cacao, honoring the sweetness and the bitterness of our struggles.

Finish with a pinch of cinnamon, for the fire that lives in our bones, the fire that will never burn out.

Drink slowly, as if savoring the waters of your ancestors, letting the warmth flow through you and remind you of the fire in your veins.

Writing Prompt:
The Revolution Runs Through Your Veins

Close your eyes and breathe deep.
Feel the rhythm of your pulse.
Listen to the beat—it's the sound of history.
It's the song of your ancestors,
rising in you like a storm.
Now, ask yourself:
What does the revolution feel like?
Is it a whisper?
A roar?

Does it move like water?
Is it in the breath you take when you speak your truth?
Is it in the hands that heal,
the hands that build,
the hands that push back against everything they said we couldn't
have?

Write freely:
What does your revolution look like?
Where do you stand in the river of it?
What parts of you need to be free?
What parts of you need to be reborn?

Meditation:
Flow Like the River

Sit comfortably, close your eyes, and breathe deeply.
Let your breath become a gentle current,
flowing in and out of your body,
moving like the river that runs through your veins.
With each breath, feel yourself being carried by the waters of history,
by the ancestors who rise with you.
Let their strength fill you.
Let their power surround you.

As you breathe, know this:
Like the river, you are unstoppable.
Like the river, you are meant to flow,
to carve your own path.
Feel the water in you,
in your blood,
in your bones.
You are the revolution.
You are the flood.
And nothing can stop your rise.

Section Two

The Return to Ourselves

Introduction:
The Return to Ourselves

We've been taught to forget, to shrink, to apologize for our
existence in a world that denies our brilliance.
But the time for forgetting has passed.
Now, we return to ourselves.
We return to the bodies that carry the stories —
stories of resilience, of rage, of resistance.
We return to our skin, our minds, our hearts,
our beauty, our brilliance, our Blackness.

In this space, we will reclaim what was stolen.
In this space, we will be unashamed.

To be Black and whole is not a crime; it is a birthright.
Let us stand in it unapologetically,
and let the world tremble in the brilliance we are meant to share.

The Sacredness of My Skin

My skin is sacred,
like the earth that birthed me,
black and deep,
like the soil, rich and full of life.
It's a map of the struggles we've survived,
the triumphs we've earned,
the love we've sown in places that never wanted to see us bloom.

Each wrinkle, a story.
Each curve, a history.
Each mark, a prayer.

My skin is sacred,
like the river,
like the sun,
like the moon.

I am a living testament to the divine,
and no one can erase my glory.

Resilience in My Bones

Do you feel it?
The weight of the generations that came before us,
the ones who marched with fire in their bellies and rivers in their
veins?
I carry their blood,
and their fire is mine.

I am not soft.
I am not fragile.
I am made of stone,
and fire,
and earth and water,

I am the strength of my ancestors ,
their resilience in my bones,
their will in my heart.

I stand tall because they stood tall.
I rise because they rose.

The Mirror Speaks

The mirror speaks,
but not in the way they told me it would.

It doesn't call me ugly.
It doesn't call me too much.
It doesn't tell me to shrink,
to hide,
to apologize.

The mirror speaks,
and it says:
You are more than enough.
You are the embodiment of beauty,
the fullness of Blackness,
the richness of the earth,
the depth of the ocean,
the fire of the sun.

The mirror speaks,
and I listen.
I have learned how to see myself,
how to love the reflection before me.

Nyah Ndidi

I want the name of my daughter
to make their tongues tremble.
Let their lips get uncomfortable,
watch them stutter, love.
Let them choke on a continent of vowels
that cannot be conquered.
Let their lips tighten,
as if calling your name pulls the sustenance right out of them.
And if they do get your name just right,
let it make them choke them on love,
for your name is the mightiest thing
their mouths will ever hold.
It took us eight days to name you, my love.
The whole world has no choice but to get it right.

Africa

I am Africa, and Africa is me!
ETHIOPIA in my spirit, KENYA in my feet.
My mother is Ausset, my sister Nefertiti.
My cousins are Nubian kings and queens.
In fiery rage, I became the Sahara.
From my eyes, tears flowed and became the Nile.
With my bare hands, I built the Sphinx,
And when that was done I crafted the Great Pyramids!
I roam with the lions— all hail Selassie,
I ride on the backs of elephants.
I am Africa, and Africa is me!
NIGER in my hair, CONGO in my teeth.
I made love to Ra, and when he filled me with his spirit,
I gave birth to civilization and named him Egypt.
He is the origin of the world's sciences and all that is sacred,
Where Aristotle, Plato, and Alexander the Great once came.
I am Africa, and Africa is me!
ANGOLA in my eyes,
SUDAN in my speech,
RWANDA in my smile,
MALI in my stride,
GHANA in my spirit,
NIGERIA in my heart!

Reclaiming the Power
of Our Bodies

Our bodies are the most sacred things we own.
In a world that seeks to commodify, abuse, and control them,
we must return to our bodies with love and reverence.

The ways we've been taught to hate our bodies,
to shrink in our skin,
to desire to be anything but what we are—
those teachings are not ours.
They were given to us by the hands of those who never
understood the sacredness of our existence.

But when we reclaim our bodies,
when we stand tall in our skin,
we are pushing back against the systems that seek to break us.
We are unlearning the lies we've been told.
We are learning to love the very thing that was once demonized,
our bodies, the temples of our ancestors.

In reclaiming our bodies, we reclaim our power.
We return to ourselves.

Recipe:
Nourish the Temple

Ingredients:

- 1 cup of hibiscus tea
- 1 tablespoon of honey
- A squeeze of fresh lime
- A pinch of cayenne pepper

Instructions:

Boil water and steep the hibiscus petals until the water turns a deep, rich red.
Add honey for sweetness, remembering the resilience of our ancestors who found sweetness even in the bitter.
Squeeze in fresh lime for clarity, for the brightness of our minds.
A pinch of cayenne pepper for fire—
the fire that runs through our veins, the fire of rebellion and love.

Sip slowly.
Feel the nourishment settle in your body.
Feel the power in every drop.
This drink is for your temple.

Section Three

Feminine Power, Sexuality, and the Sacred Body

Theme:

This section explores the complex relationship between Black women and their bodies, and how sexuality can be both a site of oppression and a profound source of spiritual and personal power. Through poems and essays, we confront the ways in which the sacred feminine has been weaponized against us, and reclaim the power and autonomy of the body as a radical act of liberation. In a world that seeks to control, subjugate, and silence the Black female body, we turn towards reverence, sensuality, and healing as acts of defiance. This is a celebration of the body as sacred, and unstoppable.

Breathless:
Love in the Time of Revolution

There are some breaths
you can only take when you're ready to fight.
And I'm not talking about no small fight,
I'm talking about a revolution.
I'm talking about holding the weight of every expectation
the world has ever thrown on us
and still finding space to breathe.

You kiss me,
and I can feel it—
not just your lips on mine,
but every truth we've both buried
pressed between our bones.
I'm talking about love
that walks into the revolution
with its fists clenched
and its heart wide open.

Love that says:
I will not break.
I will not bow.
I will not shrink.
I will stand tall
and say, *This is my body.*
This is my revolution.
I breathe because I refuse to be silenced.

So, love me like we're both free.
Like love and revolution are the same.
Like we've fought for this moment.
And I'm not just talking about us.
I'm talking about the bloodlines
that paved the way for us to take this breath,
this kiss, this fight.

Dancing in Our Skin

We dance in our skin,
don't let nobody tell you it's too much.
I know what they said,
I know what they've done.
Told us our hips were too wide
our voices too loud,
our movements too wild.

But let me tell you this:
There's power in the way we move.
Power in the way our bodies tell stories
our ancestors whispered in our ears
before they were forced to leave us.

You see, they tried to silence us,
but our bodies have always been
the loudest prayer,
the most defiant shout.
This skin is sacred,
this rhythm is divine.

We move through this world,
and the world moves out of our way.

Unforgiven

I have lived many lives in this body,
many versions of me,
and I am still learning how to forgive the past.
But you need to understand something—
I will not be sorry.
Not for the rage that lives in my blood,
not for the fire that rises in my chest
every time the world tries to silence me.

I will not be sorry
for the way I hold my body
like it's sacred,
like it's a temple of resistance,
like it's a war cry in the middle of the night.
I won't apologize for that.

You see, the truth is—
I'm not broken.
I'm not lost.
I'm not some project
for you to fix.

I am a work of art
painted with the tears of my foremothers
and the blood of my parents,
and I refuse to apologize for the strength
that comes in my bones
for the grace that comes in my voice.

I am *unforgiven*,
and I am still here.
Still breathing,
still fighting,
still loving
and I will never apologize
for being this beautiful
in a world that tried to make me disappear.

Soft Revolutions

We are not always loud.
We are not always in the street,
shouting for the world to see us,
to hear us.
Sometimes, the revolution
is in the silence.
The quiet act of loving yourself
when the world would rather you shrink.
The revolution is in the way we breathe,
the way we stand tall,
in the way we reclaim the power
that has always been ours.

You see, we don't always have to break shit
to change shit.
We can start with a smile
we can start with a touch,
we can start with a simple act of *claiming*
what is ours—
our bodies,
our hearts,
our voices.

My revolution is soft.
It is tender,
but it is powerful,
and it will not be stopped.

Sacred Touch, Sacred Fury

Do not touch me
unless you can see
the divine in me.
Don't touch me
unless you understand
that every inch of this body
is sacred—
carved by the hands of ancestors
who fought for me to stand here.

Don't touch me
unless you can feel the fury
that burns in my chest
and the tenderness that lives in my hands.
Don't touch me
unless you are ready to hold
all of me—
the softness
and the rage.

Touch me like the revolution is inside.
Touch me like my body is the land
where freedom blooms
and resistance takes root.
Touch me like you understand
that my softness
and my fury
are both holy,
both necessary.

Still I Rise:
A Black Girl's Love Song

You think my love is something soft?
Think again.
My love is steel wrapped in silk,
it is thunder,
it is light,
it is the sound of survival
and healing
in the same breath.

You think my love is a quiet thing?
No.
It's a roar.
It is the voice of every Black girl
who ever said no
and meant it.
It is the fire
that burns in my belly,
the dance that moves in my hips.

Still, I rise.
Still, I love.
Still, I take up space
and say *This is me,*
This is us,
This is our song,
and I am singing it loud.

Writing Prompts:

1. **Sacred Resistance:** Write about a time when you had to reclaim your body as sacred. What resistance did you encounter? What did that act of resistance look like, and how did it shift your perception of yourself and your power?

2. **The Power of Breath:** In moments of intense struggle or love, how does your breath change? Write a poem or essay that explores the relationship between breathing, power, and emotional release. What does your breath tell you about your strength?

3. **Soft Revolution:** Reflect on a quiet revolution you've experienced. It could be an internal shift, a small but significant act of defiance, or a moment of personal transformation. How did this revolution feel in your body? What did it teach you about strength?

4. **The Dance of Your Skin:** What does it mean to dance in your skin as a Black woman? Write about a time when you felt empowered by your body—whether through movement, expression, or simple presence. How did this act of living in your body reshape your identity?

5. **Healing Through Touch:** Write about the power of touch—both sacred and transformative. How can touch be an act of rebellion? How does it heal? Reflect on the touch of a lover, a friend, or your own self-love.

Sister, Your Body is Not for Their Consumption

They told you to shrink, to fold yourself like paper, to make yourself smaller than you are— but you didn't listen, and if you did, you are done now.

You've heard the whispers in the streets, the church, the classroom, the law— they told you your hips were too wide and your voice too loud. They told you to silence the thunder that lives in your skin. But listen, sister, you are the storm. You are the flood that waters this earth, the land where liberation blooms.

Your body is a battleground— not to be claimed, not to be tamed. It is a temple, a weapon, a revolution in motion.

So, sister, don't let them shrink you. Don't let them apologize your power. You are not their spectacle, not their object of desire or pity. You are divine.

Every curve of you, every inch of your skin is a prayer, a roar, a refusal to be erased.

This body— your body— was made for more than survival. It was made for freedom. And it will rise like the ancestors who call your name in the rhythm of your hips, in the strength of your breath, in the fire of your fury.

The Power of Unapologetic Desire:
Black Feminist Thoughts

Let's get one thing straight,
Black woman:
You are allowed to want.
You are allowed to want without shame,
without guilt,
without hesitation.
You are allowed to claim the fullness of your desire,
even if it makes others uncomfortable.
Because for too long,
they've told you that your body is a burden,
that your hunger is dangerous,
that your pleasure is offensive.
They've made you believe that your sexuality—
your unapologetic desire—
was something to be controlled,
something to be "tamed."

But I am here to tell you:
Sister, your desire is holy.
Your hunger is divine.
The way you move,
the way you breathe,
the way you love—it is sacred.
The earth can't survive without the rain,
and this world can't survive without your wildness.

Don't let them silence you.
Don't let them tame you.
You are not meant to be a shadow in this world.
You are meant to shine,
to stand in your truth,
to demand pleasure in the fullness of who you are.
Because when you do—
when you claim your power—
you release a force
so strong,
so divine,
that nothing can stop you.
Not a thing.

Breathe, Girl

Breathe, girl.
Take a deep one.
Let the air fill your lungs,
let the air fill your soul,
let it remind you
that you are alive
and every breath you take is a declaration.
A declaration of autonomy,
a declaration of liberation,
a declaration of being *unapologetically* you.
Breathe like you've been holding it in for far too long,
like you've been trying to fit in boxes they built for you,
like you've been choking on their expectations,
on their judgment.

Let that breath out,
and with it, let the shame fall away.
Let the guilt go.
Let the hurt go.
Let the history of them trying to steal your power—
let that shit go.
Breathe, girl.
And as you do,
feel the ancestors in your chest,
feel them in your ribs,
feel them in your spine,
feel them in your hips—
because this, right here,
is what they fought for.

This breath.
This moment.
This reclamation.

You are sacred.
You are not small.
You are not silent.
You are not sorry.

Writing Prompt:
Sister, Reclaim Your Sacredness

Sister,
Take a moment.
Feel your body.
I mean, really feel it.
From your fingertips to your toes,
from your lips to your hips,
feel it.
How does it move when you walk?
What does it feel like to *truly* inhabit your skin?
When was the last time you honored it?
When was the last time you praised it—just because?

Write about your body.
Write about the parts of it that make you proud.
Write about the parts of it that make you afraid.
What would happen if you let yourself be *fully* in your body?
What would happen if you walked into any room knowing that
your body was sacred,
that it was a temple,
that it was a revolution in the making?

Claim your body, girl.
Claim it with no apology.
Write about what you would do if you had the courage to stand
in it—
stand in it fully—
and demand what is yours.
Not tomorrow,
but right now.
What would that look like?

The Sacred Rage

There is rage in my bones.
Rage that echoes in the chambers of my womb,
rage that pulses with every heartbeat,
rage that rises with every breath I take.
I am angry,
and I should be.
They tried to take my body,
they tried to take my spirit,
they tried to make me *less* than what I am.
But no.
Not today.
Not anymore.

I will rage in every step I take.
I will rage in the way I love,
the way I speak,
the way I move through this world.
And that rage will be my power.
That rage will be my freedom.
That rage will be my revolution.
Because the truth is:
I was never meant to be silent.
I was never meant to shrink.
I was never meant to make myself smaller for their comfort.
I am a storm.
And I will rage.

Touch Me

Touch me like a Haitian revolution—
Bold.
Passionate.
Liberating.
Don't you dare touch me soft—
Don't you dare touch me like I'm fragile,
like my blood ain't the soil
where rebellions take root.

Touch me like fire rising from the belly of a storm,
like the thunder
that dare to speak truth
into the face of empires.
Touch me like a hymn that splits the sky
when the world forgot how to sing.
Touch me like you remember
my foremothers' names
that still echo in the sacred hollows of your tongue.

Touch me like plantains frying golden,
crackling with the sound of my joy,
the sound of my hunger
for life—
the sound of my history
deep-fried and seasoned
with centuries of revolt.

Touch me like the warmth
of my grandmamma's voice
in the kitchen,
her hands carving stories into the steam rising from her pot,

her fingers tracing the paths of ancestors you'll never know,
but you'll taste them in every bite.

Touch me like a holy mountain—
unmovable.
Untouched.
Sacred.
Touch me like you can feel the weight
of a thousand stars
and still see the divinity
carved in every curve
of my Blackness.

Touch me in your mother tongue,
don't you dare speak to me in the language
of dispossession.
Touch me like you still see me
as the moon that lights your way
and the earth that holds your feet.

Touch me like a prayer
spoken with reverence,
like a truth you are finally ready to receive,
with endurance—
with fire that will burn
forever.

Touch me—
But know this:
when you touch me,
you are not simply touching a body.
You are touching the divine.
And you will never leave
the same.

Section Four

The Reclamation of Covens and the Rise of Black Spirituality

A Black Girl Magick Manifesto

Theme: In this section, we flip the script on the long-standing myths around covens and spirituality. Forget the Westernized, white-washed version of "witchcraft"—we're talking about the *real* Black girl magic. This is about reclaiming the sacred spaces of sisterhood and community that have always existed within Black women's practices, both in the motherland and the diaspora.

It's time to throw out the old stories. We didn't need to "find" our spirituality—Black women have always been on the cutting edge of divine connection, rituals of healing, and resistance. And now, we're coming for what's ours. This section is all about reclaiming and redefining what it means to be spiritual, powerful, and unapologetically Black. We're talking about covens of resilience, circles of healing, and the magic that flows through our veins.

The Return of the Healers:
Our Magic is Not New

We were never lost. We were never without. We were never without the tools for our own liberation. The world might tell us that we are without history, without a connection to the divine. But let me tell you something—you were born from a line of women who never stopped practicing their magic.

It is not new. It is ancestral.

From the griots of the Congo to the root workers in the South, Black women have always been the healers. Whether it was in the shape of a prayer, a dance, or a potion, we have always been the ones who knew how to save ourselves. Our healing is revolutionary, our magic is sacred, and our power was never, ever given to us by anyone else. We are standing in the legacy of the mothers who never asked for permission to heal or to rise. We are those same women. And we are coming for what is ours.

Coven in the Bones

I am the witch you never thought you'd meet,
The one who whispered prayers
into the dark and made them rise.
They told me I was too loud,
too *much*,
that magic belonged to women who wear white
and speak in tongues I never learned.
I was told I had no place in the circle.
But do you know what I did?
I carved my name into the bones of the earth.
I dipped my hands into the dirt
and pulled out the history of the world—
the Blackness that spun this planet,
the Blackness that refuses to die.
I called my sisters,
I called my sisters,
we made a coven of resistance,
of rage,
of love,
and we have not stopped *rising* since.
We have always been the witches,
the healers,
the warriors,
the ones who break curses and build empires.
There's magic in the bones of a Black woman
that cannot be contained.

Sis

Sis,
Do you hear me?
I see the blood on your hands,
the dirt under your nails,
the way you hold your head up—
the way you never let them break you.
I see the way you love anyway.
The way you give when they've tried to take everything.

You walk this earth like you know
that every step is an act of defiance.
That love isn't soft,
it's steel wrapped in velvet.
Sis dont you know

You don't just heal,
you shift galaxies.

Sis,
I see you—
In every struggle,
you stand taller,
refuse to be invisible.
In every smile,
you redefine what beauty is.

Sis,
You are the future and the past,
the revolution and the song
we'll be singing for generations.
Sis, I see you,
Black, like water rising tall.

Black Girl Magic is Not an Aesthetic

You think my magic is something you can sell,
wrap up in a shiny jar and charge me to buy it?
You think it's just crystals and candles and incense?
No, baby,
my magic is older than your wildest dreams.
It's the scar on my grandmother's back
from the whip they thought would break her.
It's the hymn my mother sang
to keep me safe when they told her
I'd never survive this world.
It's the rage in my veins
and the love that sustains me.
It's the land I come from
and the roots that stretch beyond time.
Black girl magic isn't for show,
it isn't an aesthetic you can filter and post,
it is survival, it is war,
it is divinity laced in blood and bone.
My magic?
Is Black girl magic, is *me*.
It is the way I breathe when they try to suffocate my voice.
It is the way I rise when they expect me to fall.
Black girl magic is not a trend,
it's a revolution that will never end.

My Sister's Keeper

You think you know what strength looks like,
but you've never seen it in the flesh.
You've never seen the weight of the world
carried by Black shoulders
without a word,
without a flinch,
but in every step,
a revolution.

My sister—
she is Black like water.
She flows through the cracks they tried to create,
nourishing the soil,
eroding barriers with the softest touch.
She is the tide that pulls the moon,
the river that cuts through mountains,
unstoppable, unyielding,
an ocean in the flesh.

When they told us we couldn't,
we didn't whisper—we *howled*.
A sound so fierce,
it shattered glass ceilings
and burned the old world down to its knees.
And from the rubble, we rose,
we emerged like fire
from the ashes,
like water
from the depths,
reclaiming what was always ours.

My sister's keeper?
No.
She is the flood that reshapes the land.
She is the storm that won't be contained,
the current that sweeps away everything
that dares to stand in her way.
She is not here to nurture—
she's here to *transform*.
She doesn't just survive; she remakes the world
with the power of her pulse,
with the rhythm of her breath,
with the strength of her blood
that runs deep,
Black like water,
always in motion,
always reborn.

She is the creator of space
where they thought there was none.
She is the keeper of the flame
that burns brighter with every step.
She is the one who will never be dimmed,
the one whose light is a weapon,
whose voice is a weapon,
whose *existence* is a weapon.
She is the revolution that refuses to ask for permission,
that demands the world bow at her feet.

My sister's keeper?
No.
She is the keeper of legacies.
She is the keeper of the future.
She is the keeper of what they feared most:
Black womanhood, unbroken,
uncompromising,
Black like water,
rising, always rising.

Black Girl, Call Home: SOS

I resent you,
for trying to make me still,
for teaching me to shrink in spaces
meant for kings

You tried to mold me,
but I was born to break.
Not in the quiet ways you hoped,
but loud,
feral,
untamed.
You wanted me small.
I am the storm that won't be contained.

You came from the wild,
but you forgot your own roar.
You silenced your own fire,
tried to make me do the same.
But I'm fire,
I'm water,
I'm the Earth shaking in her bones.
You taught me survival,
but forgot to teach me how to live—
how to rise,
how to take up space,
how to say no
and make the world listen.

I'm done fucking folding into their tiny boxes.
Done making myself quiet for you,
for them.

Done pretending I don't carry oceans in my veins.
Done pretending I don't come from mountains.

So here's my SOS mamma:
I'm coming home to me.
I'm calling back my spirit,
the one you tried to drown,
the one you tried to shrink.
I'm feral.
I'm free.
I'm the revolution you tried to tame.
And you?
You'll have to learn how to make room.
I am the wild.
I am the flood.
I am Black like water,
and I will never be small.

Radical Herbal Recipes

Womb Fire Tea

Purpose: A tea to restore the power of the womb, increase vitality, and heal from the inside out. This recipe is for all who've felt disconnected from their body's most sacred space.

Ingredients:

- 1 tbsp dried raspberry leaf (supports reproductive health and strength)
- 1 tbsp dried red clover (for detoxifying and nourishing the body)
- 1 tsp dried ginger (for warmth and circulation)
- 1 tsp honey (to sweeten your path and heal your heart)
- A squeeze of fresh lemon (for clarity and renewal)

Instructions:

1. Bring a cup of water to a boil.
2. Steep the raspberry leaf, red clover, and ginger in the water for 5-7 minutes, allowing the tea to steep as you focus on your womb space.
3. Add honey and lemon, stirring slowly. As you drink, say aloud:
   "This body, this womb, is sacred.
   I honor my strength,
   I honor my power.
   I heal, I reclaim, I rise."
4. Drink slowly, letting the warmth flow into your body, your womb, your spirit.

The Recipe For Resistance

Purpose: To strengthen your will, boost resilience, and bring beauty and power to your spirit. This oil is for anyone in the fight—for self-love, for community, for the revolution.

Ingredients:

- 2 tbsp dried rose petals (for love, protection, and strength)
- 1 tbsp dried hibiscus (for empowerment and elevation)
- 1 tbsp dried calendula (for clarity and healing)
- 2 tbsp coconut oil (a base for deep nourishment)
- 1 tbsp castor oil (for spiritual cleansing and protection)

Instructions:

1. In a glass jar, add the dried rose petals, hibiscus, and calendula. Pour the coconut and castor oil over them.
2. Seal the jar and place it in the sun for 3-5 days, allowing the oils to soak in the power of the sun and the herbs.
3. Shake the jar every day, while repeating:
   "I call upon the strength of my ancestors,
   the love of my foremothers,
   the fire of my heart."
4. After 3-5 days, strain the herbs out and keep the infused oil. Rub it on your skin before facing any challenge, or anoint yourself to mark your spiritual protection.

Bloodroot Balm

Purpose: For protection, grounding, and banishing negative energy. This balm is sacred, ancient, and powerful—rooted in the earth, just like you.

Ingredients:

- 1 tbsp dried bloodroot (for protection and banishment)
- 1 tbsp beeswax (to seal your protection and intentions)
- 1 tbsp coconut oil (for nourishment and strength)
- A pinch of ground black pepper (for power and confidence)

Instructions:

1. In a double boiler, melt the coconut oil and beeswax together.
2. Add the dried bloodroot and black pepper into the mixture. Stir it slowly and with purpose.
3. Allow the balm to cool and set. As it hardens, speak these words:
   "I am protected.
   I am grounded.
   I banish all negativity,
   all that would harm me,
   all that would make me small."
4. Apply to the palms, forehead, and heart when you need to call upon your protection. Let it anchor you.

The Daughters of the Healers

We are the daughters of those who were cast out
but rose,
and rose,
and rose.
We are the healers—
not the kind you find in Western textbooks,
but the kind who carry the knowledge of the earth
in their skin.
Our grandmothers didn't need a degree to know
the power of the root,
the power of the herb,
the power of the tree.
They didn't need a platform to cast spells,
they had the rhythm of the universe in their hands,
and the ancestors' whispers in their hearts.
We have always been healers.
We have always known that the spirit is not separate from the
body.
We have always known that the earth will speak when we listen.
And we are here to remind you that healing is more than
a body of salves and tinctures.
It's a revolution of the soul.
It's pulling yourself back together
from the pieces they tried to scatter.
It's the reclamation of your right to be whole
and unapologetic.
We are the healers,
and we are coming to take back what was stolen.
To heal not only ourselves but the world.

The Role of the Black Feminist Witch

In a world that has tried to cast us aside, the Black feminist witch is a revolutionary. We are not the soft, passive, delicate creatures that pop culture has made us out to be. We are warriors.

We fight with magic—yes—but it is not magic that is rooted in "peace" or "passivity." Our magic is rooted in defiance. Our magic is rooted in reclamation. Our magic is rooted in *resistance*.

The Black feminist witch understands that she is the root of change. Her spells are not for entertainment. They are for survival. They are for healing. They are for dismantling every system that ever told her she didn't belong. When she casts, she *knows*. She knows she is the one, knows she is the keeper of ancient wisdom, and she knows her power is sacred.

Witchcraft is Not a Fantasy, It Is a Revolution

In this world, we are told that the only magic worth talking about is the kind that can be sold. We are told that witchcraft is a fantasy, something to be consumed by white feminists who dress in black lace and cast half-hearted spells under the glow of their indie flicks. But you and I, we know the truth. Witchcraft is not a luxury, it is not a plaything, it is a radical act of survival and self-definition.

For centuries, our magic was stolen from us. They told us we were *superstitious*. They told us we were *inferior*—that we didn't know how to live without the guidance of the very systems that sought to oppress us. They hid our power in the broomsticks of their fantasies, in the cauldrons of their lies. But our ancestors spoke the truth: Our magic was never theirs to steal.

Let me remind you: you are a descendent of healers, of women who grew herbs in the shadows of slave cabins, who spoke prayers into the wind, who danced in the moonlight and carved their power into the dirt beneath their feet. They never stopped practicing their rituals, their spells, their sacred acts of defiance. They never stopped calling upon the spirits of their foremothers, and they never stopped claiming their rightful place in this world.

This, *this* is the witchcraft that flows in your veins. The refusal to shrink, the ability to heal when no one else can, the deep knowing that even in a world designed to break you, you can still rise.

Reclaim your rituals. Reclaim your chants. Reclaim the land that was always yours to work with. You are not an outsider. You are the witch that this world has feared all along. You are the force that cannot be contained. Every time you close your eyes and call upon your ancestors, you are summoning the might of those who have always known. Your magic is not passive. It is not passive because your survival was never a given.

And the world will fear your rise. The world will fear your power. Because when Black women return to their magic, when we reclaim the coven that was stolen, they cannot deny us. And that is why we must fight—not with the tools of their oppression, but with the tools of our divine birthright.

The Power of Remembering

There is a power in remembering. It is not just an act of nostalgia, nor is it simply a mental exercise. Remembering is an act of power. It is the fierce declaration that what was stolen from us will be returned. It is a spiritual rebellion, a reclamation of what was ours, and a refusal to let anyone rewrite our story.

The world would have us forget. They would have us deny the spiritual practices that are woven into the fabric of our existence. They would have us believe that our connection to the earth, to the stars, and to the unseen forces is primitive, backward, unnecessary. But what they are truly afraid of is the power that comes when we remember.

When we remember our ancestral rituals, we remember our resilience. When we remember our sacred songs, we remember our survival. When we remember our herbs, our prayers, our dances, we tap into the wisdom of those who came before us—the ones who knew how to survive in a world that was always trying to erase them.

And so, we must remember. We must sit with our grandmothers, our mothers, our sisters, and listen to the whispers of the land, the songs of the river, the stories written in the stars. We must remember that our spirituality was never a gift granted to us by anyone else. It is ours by divine right. We are the daughters of the moon, the daughters of the earth, the daughters of the sun. We are the daughters of those who have always known the power of remembering.

To remember is to reclaim. To remember is to *resist*. And in this remembering, we find our greatest strength

Black Like Water

They don't know what it means to be Black like water.
To have the flow of rivers in your veins,
the oceans of your ancestors behind your eyes.
To carve out spaces where none exist,
to slip through cracks the world thought it sealed.

We are Black like water,
shaping the land,
cutting through mountains,
tearing down walls made of ignorance.

They thought we were fragile,
but we are the storm.
The flood that can't be contained.
The river that keeps flowing—always.
We don't stop. We rise.

Reflection:

The world would love for us to be small.
To shrink ourselves into a box that fits their narrative.
But baby, we are not made for boxes.
We are made for spaces that don't even exist yet.

The struggles we face are not just the things we survive—they are
the things that make us, that carve us out of the very earth. We rise
from the dirt, and they want to bury us in it. But they can't bury
what's made of fire. What's made of water. What's made of bone
and blood.

So yes, we bleed. We fight. We feel the weight of centuries.
But we are also the quiet revolution.
The quiet victories.
The ones who don't wait for permission.

We stand tall in the spaces they try to erase us from.
We reclaim them, and we build new ones.

Our struggles are the fire from which we are forged.
Our triumphs are the ashes we rise from.

Exercise:
Claim Your Space

Sit in a space that is yours.
Not a borrowed space. Not a small corner.
Take up the whole damn room.
Let your breath fill the air, let your spirit spread.
You are not here to shrink.
You are not here to apologize.
You are here to claim what was always yours.

Now, journal: When have you felt small? When have you felt the
weight of the world trying to make you shrink? And how did you
push back? How did you reclaim your space? Your power? Your
voice?
It's time to show up for yourself. It's time to be as loud and
unapologetic as you need to be. You're already walking in a
revolution—might as well make it loud.

Closing Reflection:

Black womanhood is a revolution in itself.
It's a revolt against the lies, the stereotypes, the narratives that try
to erase our power.

We don't just survive—
We rise.
We rebuild.
We reclaim what they took from us, and then some.

The quiet victories? The ones no one sees?
Those are the real triumphs.
Those are the spaces where our power is born.
And we carry them with us,
for the world to see,
for the world to feel.

And still, we rise.